What Happens after Death?

Basics of the Faith

Sean Michael Lucas, Series Editor

What Happens after Death?

Richard D. Phillips

P&R PUBLISHING
P.O. BOX 817 • PHILLIPSBURG • NEW JERSEY 08865-0817

The material presented here was originally published in *These Last Days: A Christian View of History*, edited by Richard D. Phillips and Gabriel N. E. Fluhrer (Phillipsburg, NJ: P&R Publishing, 2011, p. 125–148). It has been revised for this booklet.

ISBN: 978-1-59638-404-0 (pbk)
ISBN: 978-1-59638-823-9 (ePub)
ISBN: 978-1-59638-824-6 (Mobi)

Page design by Tobias Design

Printed in the United States of America

Library of Congress Cataloging-in-Publication Data

Phillips, Richard D. (Richard Davis), 1960-
 What happens after death? / Richard D. Phillips.
     pages cm. -- (Basics of the faith)
 Includes bibliographical references.
 ISBN 978-1-59638-404-0 (pbk.)
 1. Death--Religious aspects--Christianity. 2. Future life--Christianity.
I. Title.
 BT825.P48 2013
 236'.1--dc23

                    2012049748

*Even though I walk
through the valley of
the shadow of death,
I will fear no evil,
for you are with me.*
—PSALM 23:4

WHAT HAPPENS AFTER DEATH?

In 1899 two prominent men died. The first was Colonel Robert G. Ingersoll, after whom Harvard University's Ingersoll Lectures on Human Immortality are named, and who gave his brilliant mind to the refutation of Christianity. Ingersoll died suddenly that year, leaving his unprepared family utterly devastated. So grief stricken was his wife that she would not allow his body to be taken from the house until the health of the family required its removal. His remains were cremated, and his funeral service was such a scene of dismay and despair that even the newspapers of the day commented on it.

The other man who died that year was Dwight L. Moody, the great Christian evangelist. He had been declining for some time, and his family had gathered around his bed. On his last morning, his son heard him exclaim, "Earth is receding; heaven is opening; God is calling." "You are dreaming, Father," said his son. But Moody replied, "No,

Will, this is no dream. I have been within the gates. I have seen the children's faces."

Moody seemed to revive but then started to slip away again. "Is this death?" he asked. "This is not bad; there is no valley. This is bliss. This is glorious." His daughter began to pray for him to recover. "No, no, Emma," he said. "Don't pray for that. God is calling. This is my coronation day. I have been looking forward to it."

After Moody died, his funeral was a scene of triumph and joy. Those in attendance sang hymns of praise to God. "O death, where is your victory?" they exclaimed through faith in Jesus Christ. "O death, where is your sting?" (1 Cor. 15:55).[1]

The contrast between the deaths of Ingersoll and Moody not only shows the value of Christian faith, but also proves how important it is for Christians to know the Bible's teaching about death and life after death. Few of us choose to spend much time contemplating death. As a pastor, however, I often am ministering to dying people and to their families. This has caused me to reflect frequently on the Bible's teaching concerning death and dying.

One of the most important lessons I have learned is that I do not need to present to dying saints the latest scholarly exegesis of a particular passage of Scripture. Rather, people facing death most need the well-worn paths of a familiar text. Psalm 23 is a favorite passage, though certainly not the only one, for helping someone to come to grips with death.

> The Lord is my shepherd; I shall not want.
>   He makes me lie down in green pastures.
> He leads me beside still waters.
>   He restores my soul.

He leads me in paths of righteousness
   for his name's sake. (vv. 1–3)

These verses picture a believer as a sheep following the shepherd. It is a wonderful depiction of how the Lord our Shepherd cares for us in this life—and in death. Verse 4, which, I think, is still best quoted in the King James Version, reads: "Yea, though I walk through the valley of the shadow of death, I will fear no evil: for thou art with me; thy rod and thy staff they comfort me."

In this psalm, we note first that for a believer death is not the end but the middle. Death is not something *into which* we go, but something *through which* we pass. This is not normally how we think about either death in general or this psalm in particular, but, according to David, death is in the middle and what comes afterward is glorious!

This sentiment was vividly illustrated by Dr. James M. Boice, late pastor of the historic Tenth Presbyterian Church in Philadelphia. It was my privilege to be close to him as he was dying. Part of his amazing example was that, during that time, he did not look back with regret but forward with anticipation. This should be the testimony of dying Christians: saints are actually just beginning to live when they are dying!

THE BIBLICAL VIEW OF DEATH

Let us consider what the Bible says about death. First, we should note that the Bible acknowledges *the reality of death*. This runs against the grain of a culture today that strives to sugarcoat death, using expressions such as "passed away" rather than "died" or "is dead." As believers, we must face the reality of death. This is simply to speak biblically: "It is appointed for man to die once, and after that comes judgment" (Heb. 9:27).

You may be familiar with the famous resolutions of Jonathan Edwards, the majority of which he wrote at age nineteen. One of them was this: "Resolved, to think much on all occasions of my own dying and of the common circumstances which attend death."[2] What he meant was that our bodies are going to decompose and that he desired to live in light of that. It would be a great understatement to say that this kind of thinking is foreign to most modern people, never mind most nineteen-year-olds. But in Edwards's world, death, even of the very young, was a frequent occurrence. This is not commonly the case today, and so we sugarcoat death.

I may have seen more death than the average person. As a pastor, I am often around death and am reminded of Edwards's resolutions. Before being called to the ministry, I was an Army officer for thirteen years and saw a lot of death there as well. Interestingly, death affects me now much more than it used to. As Christians, we normally become more sensitive, not less, to matters of life and death. Therefore, we would all do well to heed Edwards's advice and resolve to think soberly on all occasions of our own dying. Christians are to acknowledge the reality of death; it is unhelpful for us not to do so, for the simple reason that it is foolish to live as if we are not soon going to die. This is why David prays in Psalm 39:4, "Show me, LORD, my life's end and the number of my days; let me know how fleeting my life is" (NIV).

In the second place, we must recognize *the wrongness of death*. Forrest Gump, that mediocre theologian, expressed a sentiment that many others have also shared when he said, "Dyin's just a part of livin'." This is profoundly wrong. But this kind of falsehood is not limited to Hollywood movies; it has found its way into Christian circles as well.

Consider theistic evolution, a teaching that is becoming more and more accepted by evangelicals. We should reject this teaching partly because theistic evolution is a process in which the creative engine is death. If, after beholding what he had created and pronouncing it "very good" (Gen. 1:31), God was describing a process of natural selection that includes death, then God was declaring death to be very good. But the Bible does not say death is good. Just the opposite is the case. The Bible teaches that death is the result of sin, of something evil and corrupt (Gen. 2:17; Rom. 5:12–14). Death is so wrong that Paul says, "the last enemy to be destroyed is death" (1 Cor. 15:26).

The Lord Jesus Christ himself took death seriously and considered it wrong. For example, in John 11:1–44, the apostle records the inspired history of the resurrection of one of Jesus' friends, Lazarus. We see our Lord acknowledging how grievous death is in the shortest verse of the New Testament: "Jesus wept" (v. 35). Attempts to limit the Bible's antipathy only to "spiritual death," as opposed to death in general, fail to account for the Bible's actual teaching, the example of Jesus, or the real experience of suffering people.

Bear in mind that Jesus knew his friend was going to die. In fact, when he was told that Lazarus was sick, Jesus stayed where he was two days longer (v. 6). When he arrived in Bethany and stood outside his friend's tomb, he knew full well that in a brief moment his friend would be alive again. But what did the Lord of life do? He wept. This was not just

sentimental weeping. Rather, Jesus wept because death is
offensive—that is why he was "greatly troubled" at Lazarus's
grave (v. 33). We must never be at peace with it. Notice that
Jesus did not weep over Lazarus's spiritual death—he was a
believer, after all: it was the physical death of his friend that
so outraged our Lord. In the same way, Christians should
never be reconciled to death, however comforted we may be
by Christ's conquest of it.

My father died over ten years ago, and I was very close
to him. I still find myself grieving unexpectedly at times.
People have asked me, "When are you going to get over your
father's death?"

I will get over my father's death at the resurrection and
not one minute earlier. To be sure, the Lord helps me in my
grief. But the grief is intense precisely because death is so
wrong. So let us be done with such expressions as "passed
away," as if the deceased were on vacation! No, he has suf-
fered death. He is dead. And it is a great offense.

So we see that death is both real and grievously pain-
ful. However, we must also distinguish between *the death
of the righteous* and *the death of the wicked*. Robert Shaw, a
Puritan minister who wrote a wonderful commentary on
the Westminster Confession, said this:

> There is, indeed, a vast difference between the death
> of the righteous and that of the wicked. To the latter,
> death is the effect of the law-curse, and the harbinger
> of everlasting destruction; but to the former, death
> is . . . the termination of all sin and sorrow, and an
> entrance into life eternal. To them death is divested
> of its sting, and rendered powerless to do them any

real injury. . . . It is their release from warfare, their deliverance from woe, their departure to be with Christ.[3]

This is why David wrote what he did in Psalm 23:4, which speaks of walking "through the valley of the shadow of death." Death is like a shadow for Christians. Isn't that interesting language? In the shadows, the sun cannot be seen, even though we know it is there. So also death is made in Christ to be merely a shadow for us.

When we think about how Christians pass *through* death on the way to glory, numerous Scriptures come to mind. Psalm 121:7–8 reads:

> The LORD will keep you from all evil;
>   he will keep your life.
> The LORD will keep
>   your going out and your coming in
> from this time forth and forevermore.

The psalmist is saying that the Lord will preserve the lives of Christians even in death. We find consolation in Psalm 116:15 also as we read, "Precious in the sight of the LORD is the death of his saints." In both of these psalms, and in many other Scripture verses, we see a big difference between the death of a believer and the death of an unbeliever. Only a believer can cry with Paul,

> "O death, where is your victory?
> O death, where is your sting?"

> The sting of death is sin, and the power of sin is the
> law. But thanks be to God, who gives us the victory
> through our Lord Jesus Christ. (1 Cor. 15:55–57)

Unbelievers cannot reasonably say such things.

So, as Christians, we acknowledge the reality of death. We are never reconciled to death. We know the cause of death, and we know how death is transformed for us into the gateway of life. Charles Spurgeon expressed it with these words: "Death—what is it? It is the waiting room where we robe ourselves for immortality; it is the place where the body, like Esther, bathes itself in spices that it may be fit for the embrace of its Lord."[4]

THE EXPERIENCE OF DEATH

In one of my pastorates, a deacon was diagnosed with throat cancer. For the next two years, this man endured the cycle of chemotherapy, the return of the cancer, more chemo, remission, and return until there came that dreaded medical report. There was no recourse to more chemotherapy or radiation. He and his wife came to see me with this report, and it became my duty to say: "Now let us prepare you to die." As bold as my words seemed, I felt compelled as a minister of the gospel to affirm that only the gospel can teach us how to deal with death. And both the wife and husband were gracious in their expressions of appreciation.

During the six months that I ministered to this man before his death, we met often. We had no other text but the Twenty-third Psalm. We meditated on it together. We prayed about it. We talked about it. We did this right up to the day before he died.

I will never forget how, during one of our meetings, the deacon asked, "Pastor, what's it going to be like to die?" Like many of us, he was scared of the actual experience of death.

Like everyone else who is asked that question, I had to say, "I don't know."

When it comes to death, we are all like sheep balking before a dark, shadowy canyon. Sheep do not like to go into such places. So why do they go? Because their shepherd is with them. The same is true for us: Jesus will be with us in the ministry of the Holy Spirit. His rod, a weapon for our protection, will drive off all that we fear. His staff will pull us through. Yes, the Lord our Shepherd will be with us in the valley of death.

Death is real. It is our enemy. It should be, and is, offensive to us. However, it is defeated in Christ, and Christ promises to be with us as we pass through it.

WHAT HAPPENS AFTER DEATH

Now let us turn to specific questions that many Christians (indeed, all people) have about death. Surely the most frequently asked and least understood is this: What happens to us after we die?

Let us answer by considering what happens to our bodies when we die. The Westminster Confession of Faith is very helpful on this topic. Chapter 32.1 states: "The bodies of men after death return to dust and see corruption." These Puritan ministers rightly confessed what the Bible makes so clear: At death, the soul is separated from the body.

In popular culture today, people viewing a corpse sometimes say, "He [or She] isn't there." But consider that our bodies, in a very important way, are us. We are not Gnostics or Platonists, who believe that the body is a prison from which the soul escapes. Therefore, we hold that even after death, the body remains the person. Consider John 19:40–42. Verse 40 describes Joseph of Arimathea and Nicodemus preparing "the body of Jesus" for burial. Verse 42 says, however, that they "laid Jesus" in the tomb. The body of Jesus was still Jesus.

My own father died of multiple sclerosis, which all but destroyed his body. This dreaded disease works on the body like a razor blade chopping down a big oak tree. After he died, I remember standing with the coroner, saying with tears streaming down my face: "This is my father, and death has taken him. But I will see this body resurrected in glory!"

There is a sense, however, in which we rightly say that a dead loved one is "not there" within the lifeless body. This is because, in death, our souls depart from our bodies. The soul—the conscious person, that which perceives, thinks, and experiences—is not in the body. This is what Christians ought to mean when they say, "He is not here."

When someone dies, his or her body returns to dust and sees corruption, to use Westminster's language. We see this in Scripture in verses like Acts 13:36: "For David, after he had served the purpose of God in his own generation, fell asleep and was laid with his fathers and saw corruption." In Genesis 3:19, God says to Adam, "By the sweat of your face you shall eat bread, till you return to the ground, for out of it you were taken; for you are dust, and to dust you shall return." Thus, the decomposition of the body is an effect of the fall.

But the Bible doesn't leave us there. Again, to use the Westminster Standards, answer 37 of the Shorter Catechism says this: "Their bodies, being still united to Christ, do rest in their graves till the resurrection." I love the phrase, "still united to Christ." This teaches the biblical truth that Christ knows where the bodies of all his people are and maintains his saving commitment to them.

This is why, in traditional Christian practice and out of respect for the body, the dead are buried, not cremated. (This is partly because, in the Old Testament, having one's bodily remains submitted to the flames did not reflect well on one's theological status! Let me encourage you to look up these passages: Joshua 7:25; Judges 15:6; 1 Kings 13:2; 1 Kings 16:18; 2 Kings 23:20; Isaiah 66:24. You will see what I mean about the biblical idea of cremation.) We must not be overly dogmatic on this point, because many people have cremated loved ones and the Bible does not expressly forbid this practice. Looking forward to the resurrection, however, Christians usually refrain from inflicting damage on the dead body but show reverence to it by means of burial.

We have briefly seen what happens to the bodies of the righteous when they die. But what about the souls of the righteous? Since we will all die unless Jesus returns first, we need to be very clear about what happens to our souls afterward. The fate of our bodies until Christ's return is clear from both Scripture and experience. However, there is much confusion about what happens to a believer's soul when he or she dies.

We return again to the Westminster Confession, 32.1: "Their souls, which neither die nor sleep, having an immortal subsistence, immediately return to God who gave them." This states, first, that the soul of a believer returns to God (see Luke 23:43; Eccl. 12:7). The Confession continues: "The souls of the righteous, being then made perfect in holiness, are received into the highest heavens, where they behold the face of God, in light and glory, waiting for the full redemption of their bodies" (see Heb. 12:23; 2 Cor. 5:1, 6, 8; Phil. 1:23; Acts 3:21; Eph. 4:10).

Is death an extinction of being? The answer is no. The Bible makes it clear that our souls continue to exist after death. They are disembodied but are capable of exercising those powers and faculties that are essential to them. We see this illustrated in such passages as 1 Samuel 28:1–25, which is the story of the witch of Endor. It is highly debated whether the witch conjures up Samuel or a representation of him. In any case, Saul recognizes Samuel in his state of death. Samuel speaks. He hears. He thinks. A New Testament example is found in Matthew 17:1–13, the account of Jesus on the Mount of Transfiguration. There Jesus speaks with Moses and Elijah, both of whom have been dead for quite some time! Yet their inward, conscious selves—their souls—continue to do all the things they did on earth.

A second and not unrelated question is: What about soul sleep? The Bible often says that dead people have "fallen asleep." We need to understand that this is a metaphorical description of the *body*, not the *soul*. So, yes, the Bible uses the language of sleep in reference to death, but it simply describes the appearance of one's body in the state of death. It is clear that our souls are fully active after death.

R. C. Sproul helpfully puts it in these terms: "The Bible teaches that we do not lose consciousness when we die. We will be in heaven, aware of Christ, aware of God, and aware of the other saints who are there. We will not be clothed with our resurrected bodies at that point, but we will be in an intermediate state, in which the soul exists without the body."5 So neither do we cease to exist, nor is there a soul sleep.

We have described what does *not* happen to a believer after death, so now let us turn to what *does* happen. In the first place—and this is glorious even to consider—we will be in the presence of the Lord. Second Corinthians 5:1, 6–8 says,

> For we know that if the tent, which is our earthly home, is destroyed, we have a building from God, a house not made with hands, eternal in the heavens. . . . We know that while we are at home in the body we are away from the Lord, for we walk by faith, not by sight. Yes, we are of good courage, and we would rather be away from the body and at home with the Lord.

In life, we are at home in the body and absent from the presence of God in heaven. But when we die, we are absent from the body and present with the Lord. That is why Paul says in Philippians 1:23, "I am hard pressed between the two. My desire is to depart and be with Christ, for that is far better." What did Jesus say to the thief on the cross? "Truly, I say to you, today you will be with me in Paradise" (Luke 23:43). So the souls of the just, those who are believers in Christ, justified by faith in him alone, depart from the body to be with the Lord.

With this in mind, Charles Spurgeon asked: "The grave what is it? It is the bath in which the Christian puts off the clothes of the body to have them washed and cleansed. . . . Death is the gate of life. I will not fear then to die."6 What really makes death gain is being with Christ. This is why Paul said he would rather have death if he could so choose, even though he realized that the choice was not his own to make.

So, after death, the soul of the believer retains its natural faculties. It departs from the body to the presence of the Lord, where it bathes in his glory in the highest heavens. The Confession says the soul is "beholding the glory of the Lord in light and holiness." The apostle John puts it this way: "Beloved, we are God's children now, and what we will be has not yet appeared; but we know that when he appears we will be like him, because we shall see him as he is" (1 John 3:2).

I have had the privilege of preaching through the Gospel of John. One of my favorite verses in that Gospel is chapter 17, verse 24, in which Jesus says, "Father, I desire that they also, whom you have given me, may be with me where I am, to see my glory that you have given me because you loved me before the foundation of the world." When Jesus says, "I desire," he is not merely expressing a hope. Rather, as God the Son, he is sovereignly exercising his mediatorial office, with all the rights of his fulfilled covenant. He is declaring his sovereign will for his people. We absolutely and assuredly will be with Jesus, for whatever he desires comes to pass! We will see him in the glory of his perfect humanity, and we will also see him in the glory of his deity.

Another wonderful aspect of all this is the fact that we will ourselves be perfect in holiness when we get to heaven. Here is what the author of Hebrews says:

> But you have come to Mount Zion and to the city of the living God, the heavenly Jerusalem, and to innumerable angels in festal gathering, and to the assembly

of the firstborn who are enrolled in heaven, and to God, the judge of all, and to the spirits of the righteous made perfect. (Heb. 12:22–23)

So upon our souls' entrance into heaven, we will be "made perfect." First John 1:7 says: "The blood of Jesus his Son cleanses us from all sin." We will be perfect in holiness when Christ completes our salvation. This is what Christ guarantees us.

If this is the joy that awaits the believer, what awaits the unbeliever? The Westminster Confession answers: "The souls of the wicked after death are cast into hell, where they remain in torment and utter darkness reserved for the judgment of the great day." We see this in such passages of Scripture as Luke 16:23–24, Acts 1:25, Judges 6 and 7, and 1 Peter 3:19.

In John Milton's *Paradise Lost*, the Devil says that it is better to reign in hell than serve in heaven. Many people today seem to think that the Devil does indeed reign in hell. Let me assure you, however, that nobody reigns in hell except Christ, who reigns in hell in all his terrifying power (see Heb. 10:31, Job 26:6, Ps. 139:8, and the Westminster Confession of Faith, 33.2).

What about purgatory? We must realize that the doctrine of purgatory flows of necessity from a Roman Catholic misunderstanding of the doctrine of justification. In the Catholic scheme, justification is not a declaration by God that in his sight we are righteous, once and for all, through faith alone in the finished work of Christ. Rather, Roman Catholic justification begins a process that will not gain you automatic entry into heaven when you die. Rather, the fires of purgation (hence the name) must "purge" you of your remaining sin and thus fit you for heaven.

There are many reasons to object to the doctrine of purgatory, Rome's version of the "good news." Most significant among these objections is the fact that there are no references to purgatory in any canonical book of Scripture. The author of Hebrews succinctly refutes this teaching, saying, "It is appointed for man to die once, and after that comes judgment" (Heb. 9:27).

Not only may believers in Christ trust that death will bring their spirits immediately to the presence of the glory of Christ, but they can anticipate the future resurrection of their bodies. The resurrection of the body is a necessary and glorious part of the gospel. In fact, resurrection is the experience of every believer from the moment when he or she first comes to faith. When we are born again, not only are we put right with God, but we also begin to experience the first fruits of Christ's resurrection, that is, the Holy Spirit. What does Paul say when speaking of the Spirit? He says he wants us to understand that the power that is at work in us is like the power of the Holy Spirit when God raised Jesus from the dead (Eph. 1:19–20). The Holy Spirit is resurrection power for us now, renewing us spiritually.

The resurrection is absolutely central to the gospel, both as we have a foretaste of it now in the ministry and in the presence of the Holy Spirit and also as we move toward the actual restoration of all things. Christ's resurrection begins in a believer at the moment of conversion and concludes at his return in the glorious restoration of our bodies that have died. What a resurrection hope Christians have!

THE FINAL JUDGMENT

We should note, however, that *everyone* is going to be resurrected, not just believers. Unbelievers also will be resurrected to an eternal existence. For believers, this existence will be eternal life, but for unbelievers, resurrection is to eternal death.

The resurrection of all persons will occur immediately after Christ's second coming. Immediately after this resurrection comes the final judgment. Passages like Matthew 25:31 teach this clearly: "When the Son of Man comes in his glory, and all the angels with him, then he will sit on his glorious throne. Before him will be gathered all the nations" (see also John 5:28 and Acts 24:15).

What happens to believers after their bodies are raised and rejoined to their souls? The Westminster Shorter Catechism, question 38, answers, "At the resurrection, believers, being raised up in glory, shall be openly acknowledged and acquitted in the day of judgment, and be perfectly blessed in the full enjoying of God to all eternity." At the resurrection, which takes place at the return of Christ, all who are in him will have their resurrected bodies united to their souls, subsequently to be glorified. Paul explores this in 1 Corinthians 15:42–46:

> So is it with the resurrection of the dead. What is sown is perishable; what is raised is imperishable. It is sown in dishonor; it is raised in glory. It is sown in weakness; it is raised in power. It is sown a natural body; it is raised a spiritual body. If there is a natural body, there is also a spiritual body. Thus it is written,

"The first man Adam became a living being"; the last Adam became a life-giving spirit. But it is not the spiritual that is first but the natural, and then the spiritual.

Our selfsame bodies will be raised and none other. Some of you have lost children or spouses. As a pastor, I have stood with parents over the bodies of dead children, with wives next to the body of their husbands and husbands with wives. In all such griefs, Christians will not "get over" their loss until the resurrection day, when those same beloved bodies are raised in glory and rejoined to the holy souls of our redeemed friends. I often have reminded grieving Christians over the bodies of loved ones who have died: "Those hands will hold your hands again! That dear voice will be heard again! This body in Christ will not be defeated but will have the victory in his resurrection! Death will not prevail, even over this mortal flesh!" In the great day of Christ's glorious coming, "the mortal [will put] on immortality" (1 Cor. 15:54). What a hope Christians have in the resurrection of the body!

After our bodies are raised, believers will also be acknowledged by Christ. Matthew 25:34 teaches: "Then the King will say to those on his right, 'Come, you who are blessed by my Father, inherit the kingdom prepared for you from the foundation of the world.' " Isn't this wonderful? Jesus will acknowledge us as belonging to him, as having a right to enter his kingdom and his glory. Notice as well that he brings us to himself—"Come, you who are blessed by my Father." Christ is himself, together with the glory of the Father, the chief glory and blessing we receive at his return.

Having been acknowledged as his own, believers will also be acquitted by Christ. This is a controversial subject these days, when one hears about "a future justification according to works." Advocates of a teaching known as the New Perspective on Paul (and others) teach that while we are justified by faith now, what really determines whether we "make it" in the end will be our works of obedience. They point to passages like Matthew 25 in an attempt to argue this view. But notice that when Jesus sits on his throne and separates the just and the unjust, they are already distinguished as "sheep and goats." The "sheep" do not appear in order to be judged with the "goats" but are separated prior to the final judgment.

Believers appear at the final judgment as those already fully justified. Yes, they must be acquitted, but their acquittal is no more in doubt than the distinction between their status as sheep and the status of the unjust as goats. Moreover, we should realize that believers appear at the final judgment already having entered into the reward of justification and already having entered into glorification in the form of glorified resurrected bodies. This is why Paul refers to Christ's coming as "our blessed hope" (Titus 2:13). Christians do not learn on the final day whether or not they will be justified based on their performance. Instead, the justification we have received by faith alone in this life is consummated in our resurrection and confirmed by our acceptance into Christ's glory.

Moreover, having been acknowledged and acquitted by Christ, believers will experience the eternal enjoyment of God. John's vision in Revelation 21:3–5 sums up what this will mean for all who belong to Christ:

> And I heard a loud voice from the throne saying, "Behold, the dwelling place of God is with man. He will dwell with them, and they will be his people, and God himself will be with them as their God. He will wipe away every tear from their eyes, and death shall be no more, neither shall there be mourning nor crying nor pain anymore, for the former things have passed away."
>
> And he who was seated on the throne said, "Behold, I am making all things new."

For believers, the future resurrection involves the raising and glorifying of our bodies as they are reunited with our souls, the open acknowledgment that we belong to Christ, our full and final acquittal in Christ, and our being brought into the eternal enjoyment of God. How much we have to look forward to after death and in the return of Jesus. No wonder David rejoiced: "You anoint my head with oil; my cup overflows. Surely goodness and mercy shall follow me all the days of my life, and I shall dwell in the house of the LORD forever" (Ps. 23:5–6).

We should note a few more points about the final judgment. No one knows the day, but God has appointed it. "God has appointed a day," says the Westminster Confession, 33.1, "wherein he will judge the world in righteousness, by Jesus Christ, to whom all power and judgment is given of the Father." God will judge the earth in the person of the God-man, in the person of his Son, who is best fitted to render perfect judgment on mankind (see Acts 17:31 and John 5:27). The final judgment is, therefore, a fixed, appointed day, the timing of which is known only to God (Matt. 24:36).

Regarding the judgment itself, the Westminster Confession says: "In which day, not only the apostate angels shall be judged, but likewise all persons that have lived upon the earth shall appear before the tribunal of Christ to give an account of their thoughts, words, and deeds; and to receive according to what they have done in the body, whether good or evil" (33.1). Didn't we just say that this judgment is not according to works? Is the Confession saying something different here? No. Let's look at why this is the case.

First of all, the final judgment will be a just judgment. It will be a righteous judgment. A. A. Hodge wrote, "It is a dictate of natural reason and conscience that in some way, formally or informally . . . God will call all the subjects of his moral government to an exact account for their character and actions."[7] Hodge further reasons that since God's justice must hold sway, and since this has not yet fully happened, there must be perfect justice in the final judgment.

Who will be the subjects of this judgment? The answer is apostate angels and all persons (see Jude 6 and Heb. 9:27). What about them will be judged? The Confession answers: "All their thoughts, words, and deeds, what they have done in the body, whether good or evil" (see Eccl. 12:14, Matt. 12:36, and Rev. 20:12). According to Revelation 20:12, in the final judgment books reveal every thought, action, or desire: "Books were opened. . . . And the dead were judged by what was written in the books, according to what they had done."

If this is true, how can Christians escape this judgment, since we too have sinned? The answer is found in John's statement that "another book was opened, which is the book of life." He adds, "If anyone's name was not found written in the book of life, he was thrown into the lake of fire" (Rev. 20:12, 15). According to the Bible, the deeds of those who rejected Christ will be exposed and punished with everlasting judgment. Believers, in contrast, find their names in another book, the book of life. Revelation 13:8 mentions this same book, calling it "the book of life of the Lamb that was slain."

The book of life is the book of the life of Jesus Christ. Believers are "judged," then, according to the perfect righteousness of Christ, which is imputed to them through faith, their own sins having already been judged on the cross where Jesus died. Realizing this, Christians have nothing to fear in the final judgment. If you have believed in Jesus for salvation, your name has been graciously placed in the book of life, just as your sins have been punished forever on the cross. You will therefore be judged according to the works of another—the righteous works of Jesus Christ—and you will be admitted into the eternal glory of your Lord.

One additional observation comes from Jesus' important description of the final judgment in Matthew 25:34–40. Jesus speaks in praise of the good works of his people, not as the basis of their justification but as a further instance of his grace:

> Then the King will say to those on his right, "Come, you who are blessed by my Father, inherit the kingdom prepared for you from the foundation of the world. For I was hungry and you gave me food, I was thirsty and you gave me drink, I was a stranger and you welcomed me, I was naked and you clothed me, I was sick and you visited me, I was in prison and you came to me." (Matt. 25:34–36)

Our sins have been punished once and for all on the cross, and the righteousness of Christ has been imputed to us for justification. The Lord then rewards the good works we did by God's grace. Here is the judgment of believers of which Paul speaks in 2 Corinthians 5:10: "Each one may receive what is due for what he has done in the body, whether good or evil." Our evil has already been punished, and now our good works are rewarded on the threshold of the new and eternal age.

What is fascinating about this scene is that the righteous are surprised that Jesus is commending them:

"Then the righteous will answer him, saying, 'Lord, when did we see you hungry and feed you, or thirsty and give you drink? And when did we see you a stranger and welcome you, or naked and clothe you?'" Jesus will answer, "Truly, I say to you, as you did it to one of the least of these my brothers, you did it to me" (Matt. 25:37–40).

Note that Jesus notices and rewards activities that we would not typically consider really weighty. Jesus does not say, "You translated the Bible into a foreign language. You planted fourteen churches. You raised millions of dollars for charity." Of course, these are not bad things at all! But here Jesus commends the daily love, the daily ministry, the simple service, and the quiet care of his people. We might overlook these kinds of things now, but Christ does not. So the only surprise for the righteous in heaven is that Jesus noticed and cared so much about our involvement in just being his servants, doing our best to live for him. It will amaze us then how much our simple, daily ministry—all that we do for others because we love Jesus—means to him now.

HEAVEN AND THE ETERNAL STATE

There are other questions that people typically have about heaven and the eternal state. Where will heaven be in the end? The Bible's answer is that it will be right here on earth. The Bible does talk of a place where disembodied souls are prior to Christ's return. But after the resurrection and the renewal of the cosmos, the universe will be born again. The eternal glory will not be "all new things" but "all things new." The earth will be reclaimed, and the cosmos will be reborn. Paul writes that "the creation itself will be set free from its bondage to decay and obtain the freedom of the glory of the children of God" (Rom. 8:21). We will dwell in glorious, resurrected bodies in a garden-temple that will make the original garden pale by comparison.

What will we do in heaven? We will worship. Revelation 7:15 says, "They are before the throne of God, and serve him day and night in his temple." And we will work. Does that surprise you? It shouldn't, for we were made by God to worship and work. Donald Macleod writes, "The re-creation of the universe will involve a republication of the creation mandates to subdue and replenish the earth (Gen. 1:28)."[8] We struggle now with work because we work under a curse. But think about this: What do you like to do? What are your hobbies? Don't you enjoy those things? Isn't that why you do them? In heaven, the work that God gave Adam to do in the first garden will continue all through the cosmos, unstained by the frustration of sin, and we will commune in the worship of our Creator God. The worship and work of the eternal age in glory will be such that the Bible refers to its experience as the "rest" of our souls (Rev. 14:13). Here is the great Sabbath in full consummation: the true and final *shalom*, the worship and work for which we were originally intended and in which we receive eternal satisfaction before the face of God.

Lastly, who will be there? John writes these words in Revelation 7:13–14:

> Then one of the elders addressed me, saying, "Who are these, clothed in white robes, and from where have they come?" I said to him, "Sir, you know." And he said to me, "These are the ones coming out of the great tribulation. They have washed their robes and made them white in the blood of the Lamb."

Those who pass through the great tribulation will be in heaven. That is not a reference to a set period of time at the end of the age. John is speaking primarily about the world we're living in. We pass through it and all its trials, and we wash our robes in the blood of the Lamb.

The gospel goes forth to you today. It says that whoever will come to Jesus for salvation and eternal life, let him come. Take the free gift of the water of life. Believe in the Lord Jesus Christ. If our study of life after death shows anything, it shows that it is absolutely imperative that you should believe in Jesus. Wash your robes. Make them white in the blood of the Lamb.

If you do not, I think the words of Aragorn, in the film adaptation of J. R. R. Tolkien's *The Fellowship of the Ring* are appropriate. When he sees the ringwraiths coming for Frodo, he asks the young hobbit, "Are you frightened?" Trembling, Frodo answers, "Yes." Aragorn looks at him and says, "Not nearly frightened enough."9

But if you turn to Christ in faith, you have every reason to stop fearing death and start preparing for it with the glorious hope of eternal life.

NOTES

1 Richard D. Phillips, *Hebrews Reformed Expository Commentary* (Phillipsburg, NJ: P&R Publishing, 2006), 467.

2 Jonathan Edwards, *Jonathan Edwards' Resolutions and Advice to Young Converts*, ed. Stephen J. Nichols (Phillipsburg, NJ: P&R Publishing, 2001), 18.

3 Robert Shaw, *The Reformed Faith* (repr., Inverness: Christian Focus Publications, 1974), 400.

4 Charles Haddon Spurgeon, *Spurgeon's Sermons* (Grand Rapids: Baker Book House, 1999), 1:229.

5 R. C. Sproul, *Truths We Confess* (Phillipsburg, NJ: P&R Publishers, 2006–2007), 3:177.

6 Spurgeon, *Spurgeon's Sermons*, 1:229.

7 A. A. Hodge, *The Confession of Faith* (repr., Edinburgh: Banner of Truth Trust, 1958), 390.

8 Donald Macleod, *A Faith to Live By: Understanding Christian Doctrine* (Fearn, Ross-shire, UK: Mentor, 2002), 330.

9 "The Nazgûl," *The Lord of the Rings: The Fellowship of the Ring: Four-Disc Special Extended Edition*, directed by Peter Jackson (2001; New York, USA: New Line Home Video, 2002), DVD.

ALLIANCE®

OF CONFESSING EVANGELICALS

What is the Alliance?

The Alliance of Confessing Evangelicals is a coalition of confessional pastors, scholars, and churchmen proclaiming biblical doctrine in order to foster a Reformed awakening in today's church. Our members join for gospel proclamation, biblically sound confessional doctrine, fostering of reformation, and the glory of God. We work and serve the church through media, events, and publishing.

The work started in media—*The Bible Study Hour* with James Boice, *Every Last Word* featuring Philip Ryken, and *Dr. Barnhouse & the Bible* with Donald Barnhouse. These broadcasts air daily and weekly throughout North America, as well as online at AllianceNet.org.

reformation21 is our online magazine—a free "go-to" theological resource. Our online daily devotionals include *Think and Act Biblically* and *Making God's Word Plain*, as well as MatthewHenry.org, a resource fostering biblical prayer.

Our events include the Philadelphia Conference on Reformed Theology, the oldest continual, national Reformed conference in North America, and regional events including theology and Bible conferences. Pastors' events, such as Reformation Societies, continue to encourage, embolden, and equip church leaders in pursuit of reformation in the church.

Alliance publishing includes books from a list of trustworthy authors including titles such as *Zeal for Godliness*, *Our Creed*, and more. We also offer a vast list of affordable booklets, as well as eBooks such as *Learning to Think Biblically* and *How to Live a Holy Life*.

The Alliance further seeks to encourage sound, biblical doctrine by offering a wide variety of CD and MP3 resources featuring Alliance broadcast speakers and many other nationally recognized pastors and theologians.